FORGETTING MY F

Jill Abram grew up in Manchester, travelled the world and now lives in Brixton. Her poems have been published widely and she has performed them across London and beyond, including at Ledbury, StAnza, and Verve Poetry Festivals and in Paris, New York, Chicago and online. She produces and presents a variety of poetry events, including the Stablemates series of poetry and conversation, and was Director of the influential collective Malika's Poetry Kitchen for 12 years . jillabram.co.uk

Forgetting My Father

Jill Abram

Broken Sleep Books

ISBN: 978-1-915760-12-8

Cover designed by Aaron Kent

Edited and typeset by Aaron Kent

Broken Sleep Books Ltd   Broken Sleep Books Ltd
Rhydwen   Fair View
Talgarreg   St Georges Road
Ceredigion   Cornwall
SA44 4HB   PL26 7YH

Contents

i.m. Leo Abram

לייב בן ר׳ יוסף יצחק

1922 – 2012

Loved and Missed

Like A Fiddler on the Roof

My grandfather came from a shtetl in The Pale –
Anatevka. Maybe. I never knew his stories, adopted
those of Tevye the Dairyman. At the end of the movie,
expelled from their *intimate, obstinate, dear little village*,
the Jews go on foot to find landsleit and safer places,
books and shabbas candlesticks carried in baskets and cases,
heads covered in hats or scarves, shawls across backs.

Last summer, the news showed a colourful straggle
walking through Hungary, holding plastic bags
and mobile phones, alongside cars and trucks
on multilane motorways, past rolls of razorwire,
under gantries with signs to hoped-for places.
It did not show whether they reached Vienna,
whether they walked all the way, were welcomed.

How To Belong

At Jewish youth club we all wore
Rock Against Racism badges
and danced to *Glad To Be Gay* -
girls in one ring, boys in another.

They ate ham sandwiches when
their parents weren't looking yet
scorned me for Smokey Bacon crisps
and going to school on Yom Kippur.

The Evangelicals lured us into their
church hall with ping pong then tried
to keep us with singing and prayers
and Jesus. They wanted all of us.

We Used The Back Door

Her bosom met her belly
and the ornaments rattled
as she waddled past, glancing
at the mezzuzah on the door frame.

She went to shul to pray,
not to gossip or show off her new hat
and she walked there from home,
not from the car hidden around the corner.

We played with her visiting grandchildren
but went to see her when they weren't there,
even when our grandma brought chocolate
on Sundays we preferred to be with theirs.

She had dark circles around her eyes
though she deserved the sleep of the just.
Surely heaven is for all good people,
not just those who believe in Jesus.

Inheritance

A coat, a jacket, five pairs of knickers and Alfred –
my grandmother's legacy to me; the bronze tortoise
which I still see hiding in the hairs of the hearthrug
at Woodlea, opposite the park on Wythenshawe Road.

My sister has silver grape scissors, an eternity ring
and the canteen of cutlery. There's a red pyrex bowl
in Mum's cupboard filled with memories of custard.
My aunt liked the ugly paintings, she got them all.

Grandma didn't leave a will with lawyers. She left
a locked deed box in her flat and dozens of keys
which didn't fit. We broke it open. It was stuffed
with letters: *My dearest Bessie ... forever your Sim.*

At My Mother's Knee

Just half a cup for me, please.
At home Mum drinks tea from a pot poured through a strainer
into a cup and saucer. At my sister's it's a bag in a mug, a slug
of milk, stirred, squeezed, filled to the top. *Drink what you want,
leave the rest.* Mum dislikes waste; fledged in the fifties,
more Austerity than the New Look. There are tins in her larder
dating back decades, twelve year old quiches in her freezer.
She thinks if you don't open the carton, cream will keep
for months. If she's wrong, she'll bake a batch of scones.

She dressed us in home-made outfits and hand-me-downs.
My bike came ready-rusted, our piano was second hand,
only cheap brands in our house, no state-of-the-art for us.
As adults, my sister showed me you can throw things out;
leftovers, wrapping paper, yoghurt pots, clothes not worn
for so long you can count it in fractions of a century.
I worked out for myself cling film could be used just once
but when we visit my sister, I take Mum's full mug of tea
and tip out half a cup for me.

My Sister Is

a gold coin:
She is precious.
Her style is simple and elegant.
I'd like to exchange her
for something of equal value.

an alarm clock:
Controlled by radio from Rugby,
accurate to a fraction of a second.
If she were by my bed, she'd go wrong
and wake me at 5am.

a mid-morning beverage:
Green tea fits her philosophy,
black coffee her personality.

a steamroller:
She'd say that was more appropriate
for me, being heavier than her.
I'd say she has a greater power to crush.

a bear:
Will she be a ferocious, mama grizzly
or cuddly teddy? We never know
until she gets here.

a window:
Round, square or arched?
Hmm, certainly arch

a hand thrown pot:
Finest china drawn out thin, glazed
in lustrous copper and cobalt. In the kiln,
a bubble formed on her rim.

a coffin:
Made to measure, lined with silk,
a velvet cushion, and no shortage
of people to carry it.

Father Tongue

The sweetest naartjies I ever ate
were bought on the roadside
from a barefoot boy in tatty shorts
and a T shirt with a hole below *Man U*.

He looked younger than me at ten –
I couldn't believe he'd seen my home team
even though I'd flown eighteen hours
to where he and my Dad were born.

He took Dad's coin with both hands
and a smile which lifted his eyes.
He waved at me as we drove away slowly
so our wheels didn't spit dust over him.

Whenever I peel a tangerine I see him.
I let juice linger in my mouth while
I consider the Afrikaans word I never heard
in England, except in our house.

At Rest

In what used to be your garden, a hammock lolls
between two trees. All afternoon I swung to thoughts
of you, how you tried to teach me to hit a golf ball.

You bought two rubber dinghies for three daughters.
We found ways to share; sailed single-handed
then doubled up, an oar each or captain and crew.

When I needed crutches to keep up with them
on sand, I gained equality at sea, powered by
my arms or surfing waves back to the beach.

At night, I'd drift off to sleep
feel again the sea lapping,
the boat bobbing.

Another Time, Another Place

I picked figs and plums off the trees in Auntie's garden
and popped them straight into my mouth.
I played in her swimming pool with my sisters,
fought my big boy cousin for the inflatable chair.

I don't know who lives there now – her son
is across an ocean, we're on another continent.
My Dad, the last of their generation, lives
even further away, in a world of his own.

Our Father

We prayed every weekday morning.
                              I'll rephrase:
In assembly we recited the Lord's Prayer.
When I listened to the words I became selective;
kept the daily bread and forgiveness, stopped
hallowing his name.
                    Grandma once tempted me
to shul with sweets. Even the promise of wine
at the kiddush can't get me there now.
                                    But when
Dad was in a coma and I was impotent
and the doctors just said *Wait*
                        I cried out
for divine intervention. He came round,
damaged – I should have let the Spirit (who knows
what we ought to pray for) make intercession
with groanings too deep for words.

(Romans 8:26)

Words Are Not All We Have

Words are all we have.
— Samuel Beckett

Don't get into debt with anyone but me!
Dad's sole instruction when he left me
at university. When we did the reckoning
he took the hit on my car's depreciation.
And because I'd sold it, he drove 300 miles
in his to bring me and all I owned home.

We argued over SI units once. I fetched all
my A-level text books, showed him proof
after proof. He wasn't having it. He'd grown up
with imperial; I knew metric, and that I was right.
Next day he brought a page he'd found at work,
looked at the floor as he handed it to me: *I withdraw.*

Now he can't say anything because of the tube
in his throat and maybe – we'll know when they
remove it – that blood clot. When I try to leave
his bedside, he grips my finger and won't let go.

Marriage Vow

Mum says Dad was brought as a date for her sister
by his friend who said, *This is my friend Leo.*

Mum says Dad would have asked out whoever answered the phone,
but he only rang at dinnertime when she was nearest.

Mum says Dad took her to dinner and concerts,
If I wanted to have fun, I'd go out with one of the others.

Mum says Dad said, *I'd like to marry you,*
but I only earn £4 a week.

Mum says Dad went away so when he came back
she said, *I suppose we'd better get married.*

Other people said she could give up work once
she was a wife but Dad said, *Not bloody likely!*

After more than fifty years and two more generations
Dad says, *Turn the radiator up, I can't hear a word!*

Dad says, *Have I had my dinner?* when he's just had his lunch.
Mum says *We've had the better, now's the worse.*

Leaving

After he woke, but before he could speak,
he held my finger in a baby-strong grip
so I couldn't leave, smiled with his whole face
so I wouldn't leave, and when I said
He could wiggle his ears, he wiggled them
to show me he was still there.

Before this were monitors, tubes, a hole
in his throat, hiss-clunking vent, a blurred
scan of his brain because the dark patches
made him thrash about, and so the sedation,
coma, and the Scottish consultant who said
Another infection could carry him away.

He asked if I could see plane wreckage
through the window, if he'd killed Mum
in a car crash – forgot he'd seen her earlier.
He spent an afternoon organising a conference
from his private room with ensuite, worried
there wouldn't be enough wine for the dinner.

Now he speaks to me with old-style respect.
He's polite but I miss his teasing – he should
pat my bottom or tickle me out of a hug.
I fasten his coat, I take him to the toilet.
I wish away the time till his supper is served
so I can leave without a leave-taking.

The Longest Bereavement

We only get glimpses of him these days:
What do you want me to do – yump for yoy?
A family phrase when Mum complains
he doesn't seem pleased to see her.

He usually remembers my name
and can still go out, if we take him,
but forgets where he's been,
and then that he went.

The start of his departure was so long ago.
Then, he'd ask, *What are you doing
this afternoon?* three times during lunch.
Today he asks with each forkful.

Many Happy Returns

Where's my brother? *He's in South Africa.*
So what's this place? *Eventhal House.*
Who lives here? *You live here, Dad.*
Who are you? *I'm your daughter.*
Who's your mother? *She is.*
Does she live here? *No, she lives in Gatley.*
So what's this place? *Eventhal House.*
Where's that? *Manchester.*
Manchester? *Yes, Manchester.*
Who are you? *I'm your daughter.*
Where do you live? *London.*
London? *Yes, London.*
Why are you here? *To visit you.*
What are we doing? *Celebrating your birthday.*
Is it my birthday? *Yes.*
How old am I? *87.*
87? *Yes.*
I'm 87? *Yes, Happy Birthday!*
I'm 87! I'd better sit down.

'Peace-parted Souls'

I remember Sydney sweating from sun and exertion
    as he chased his great-nieces around the garden
        before he was too frail to walk without a stick.

I remember Ysabel filling her house
    with four generations of family and aromas of chicken soup
        before she had to lie on the floor to ease her pain.

I remember Cyril driving placidly to family picnics
    ignoring the playful screams of his daughters in the back
        before his illness confined him to the house.

I remember Martha as the life and soul, drinking pints
    and making mischief before her disease stopped
        her singing, cycling and seeing friends.

I remember Harriet dancing and flirting,
    men flocking and falling at her feet before the tumour
        took her eyesight and the treatment took her hair.

And I remember Dad when he still remembered me,
    when we argued over principles of physics and crossword clues
        before he had Velcro on his shoes instead of laces.

Anno Domini

A sunlit, summer evening.
Three little girls dance
to a bargain bin single
in their pyjamas on the patio
where Mum irons to keep
extra heat from the house.
She smooths clothes
to the rhythm of the song.
Dad won't be tempted
from his favourite armchair
in the corner of the lounge.

Dad's chair. His place.
The carpet at his feet wore out –
patched. Upholstery faded –
replaced. A new, plump cushion
before his bones rested on wood.
In time, the old one reinserted
to ease his rising. Now
the chair stays empty.
No one likes to sit in it, they never did;
But when I visit, I sit there.
Not to replace but to remember.

I Have Forgotten My Father

I have forgotten he could perform miracles;
packing luggage for a family of five's week
in Wales into the boot of a Vauxhall Victor,
that he would dig cars in the sand for me to drive
steering with a bucket, changing gears with a spade,
how he would lift and throw me over the waves.

I have forgotten that one morning he woke me
in the dark to take the train to London where I pressed
all the buttons in the Science Museum and ate two eggs
and chips for lunch; that when Princess Anne got married
so school was closed he took us to the Lake District
and made a surprise detour to Blackpool Illuminations.

I have forgotten he played Thompson's First Piano Duets
with my sister, squeezed together on one stool –
he always took the bass line so she could have the tune;
how he made me feel grown up by asking me to choose
his ties, making me his golf caddy, letting me
listen to the Man Talk; that I had the first

Walkman in the North West which he brought me
from Hong Kong; that he excused himself from a banquet
in China to ring me on my birthday before returning
to teach his Chinese colleagues to disco dance,
drink them under the table with Mao Tai and fax
for the next man out to bring him more Yorkie bars.

I have forgotten his capital cities quizzes during dinner,
how he would pluck radishes from the salad bowl but
told us to *Do as I say, not as I do!* if we tried to pick out
cucumber; that he wouldn't eat curry, but liked horseradish
and English mustard, and had to have ice cream twice a day.
It's never too cold for ice cream! he used to say.

Slow Orphaning

Images slide across my lock screen at random:
hot pink rhododendrons at Kew last May,
glasses of rum and ginger on a hotel balcony.
Here's Mum, pensive and beautiful as she
gazes at the skyline from a Thames boat
when she came to see me. The last time
I tried to visit her, she said she was busy.

Dad teeing up on the ninth at Dunham
in an orange cagoule. Rain never held him back.
A heart attack slowed him. A bypass stopped him
at a stroke. His body survived fifteen years
while his mind died and I grieved for
so long. So long I was surprised
there were still tears for his funeral.

Rites of Passage

With 18 candles burning, an uncle picks
a good key on the piano
and a family sings to you. A grandma holds
your hair from the flames

as you lean over the cake she baked
to make a wish.
Glass doors open to let the sun in,
some nieces out –

they sit on the ping pong table in the garden
as some brothers try
to play. A mum and dad chop vegetables
side by side,

two sisters compare notes on raising children,
two aunts look
at photographs while you use your gift
to take more.

Only the Grandad isn't here. He hasn't been here
for a long time.
But on this day when you come of age, today
at least he is somewhere else.

Avelut

i) Next Day
Scents of damp earth and wool
hang in the air, mingle with salt.
An arm around my shoulders,
murmurs in a language I don't understand.
Off the path, heels sink,
ropes lower the coffin.

ii) Unveiling
Today is for memories, not mourning.
Recalling the good times,
which left so long before he did,
elicits some tears.
The cloth is pulled off
dark grey granite.

iii) Yahrzeit
Another September Sunday,
a sunny one and the family
is together again, celebrating.
Nineteen candles on a cake
for his granddaughter to blow out,
one left burning.

In Judaism, Avelut *is the year of mourning after burial of a parent,*
Yahrzeit *is the anniversary according to the Hebrew calendar.*

Widow-wife

She consulted with other doctors
on how to fix Dad's heart,
visited intensive care twice daily,
even while he was unconscious.

Back home, a slow shift from
supervision to clock-round vigilance
until a week of respite care –
she started to thaw out on day three.

She crossed town every weekend
to his care home, stitched name tags
in his clothes, which still went missing
so she didn't recognise his outfits

and soon he didn't recognise her.
She'd sneak in non-kosher chocolate
and reunite him with his own stick
so he could walk without a stoop.

His carers said they'd nurse him
but a nurse said he could be treated
and ignored the DNR she'd signed
to let him die in peace.

She goes to Bridge Club, visits her
penpal in Paris, flies Business Class
to Australia. She has a new hip.
His stick stands by the front door.

Mythos and Logos

If you told me I wasn't sitting at this table on a spring day,
pen to paper writing this, occasionally looking out past
the cat sprawled on a warm paving stone in the yard, and
budding leaves twinkling like fairy lights in the sunshine
to walkers in his'n'hers Gore-Tex poling down the valley,
a pheasant couple playing peepo among clumps of grass,
a sheep squatting in the lee of a boulder suckling a lamb,
and a two-carriage train slicing the hillside from right to left
one hour, left to right the next, I'd think you were mad.

And if Dad thought he was in an ensuite hotel room, asking
me the way to the beach, until he realised Mum wasn't there
so it must be a work trip, and instead told me about the paper
he would deliver at the conference, then who am I to tell him
he's in a hospital bed, that he'd spent weeks with machines
labouring to give respite to his clogged lungs, that it was only
half an hour since Mum left and she'd be back tomorrow?

And now, you can't convince me that the fox which trots
past my gate at the same time every night as I slide the bolt
and pull the curtain across the front door is not my father
on late patrol, checking his darling daughter is home safe.
And why would you want to?

Acknowledgements

With thanks to my many, many friends in Poetry World – fellow poets and inspiring teachers. There aren't enough pages to mention you all, but I have to name the Malika's Poetry Kitchen family especially Peter, Katie, Michelle and Hannah; Jane Draycott and the Tideway Poets; Mimi Khalvati, Jo Bell, Kim Moore, Mona Arshi, Kathy Pimlott, Sophie Herxheimer, Mary Mulholland, and the One Submission a Month Facebook group. Thanks also to the editors who have given me pages, the programmers who have given me stages and my publisher, Aaron Kent at *Broken Sleep Books*.

I have huge appreciation for the friendship and support of Penny & Mark, Rosie & Martin and Maggie & Rupert. I couldn't have written these poems without my family, whom I hope won't notice some of the liberties taken with their stories.

The following poems (or versions of them) have been previously published:
Father Tongue in *Harana Poetry*
How to Belong in *Bread Poetry*
Leaving was Highly Commended in the Liverpool Poetry Prize
Like A Fiddler on the Roof in *Tears in the Fence*
Many Happy Returns in *Domestic Cherry*
Marriage Vow in *Cake*
and **Rites of Passage** in *Poetry Wales*

LAY OUT YOUR UNREST

Milton Keynes UK
Ingram Content Group UK Ltd.
UKHW011822080823
426542UK00002B/3